The History

Of The

Dionysian Artificers

A FRAGMENT

BY

HIPPOLYTO JOSEPH DA COSTA, ESQ.

THE mysteries of the ancients, and the associations in which their doctrines were taught, have hardly been considered in modern times, but with a view to decry and ridicule them.

The systems of ancient mythology have been treated as monstrous absurdities, debasing the human reason, conducting to idolatry, and favouring depravity of manners.

However, they deserve attention, if the motives of their inventors, rather than the profligacy and ignorance of their corruptors be contemplated.

When men were deprived of the light of revelation, those who formed systems of morality to guide their fellow creatures, according to the dictates of improved reason, deserved the thanks of mankind, however deficient those systems might be, or time may have altered them; respect, not derision, ought to attend the efforts of those good men; though their labours might have proved unavailing.

In this point of view must be considered an association, traced to the most remote antiquity, and preserved through numberless viscissitudes, yet retaining the original marks of its foundation, scope, and tenets.

It appears, that, at a very early period, some contemplative men were desirous of deducting from the observation of nature, moral rules for the conduct of mankind. Astronomy was the science selected for this purpose; architecture was afterwards called in aid of this system; and its followers formed a society or sect, which will be the object of this enquiry.

The continuity of this system will be found sometimes broken, a natural effect of conflicting theories, of the alteration of manners, and of change of circumstances, but it will make its appearances at different periods, and the same truth will be seen constantly.

The importance of calculating with precision the seasons of the year, to regulate agricultural pursuits, navigation, and other necessary avocations in life, must have made the science of astronomy an object of great care, in the government of all civilized nations; and the prediction of eclipses, and other phenomena, must have obtained for the learned in this science, such respect and veneration from the ignorant multitude, as to render it extremely useful to legislators, in framing laws for regulating the moral conduct of their people.

The laws of nature and the moral rules deducted from them were explained in allegorical histories, which we call fables, and those allegorical histories were impressed in the memory by symbolical ceremonies denominated mysteries, and which, though afterwards misunderstood and misapplied, contain systems of the most profound, the most sublime, and the most useful theory of philosophy.

Amongst those mysteries are peculiary remarkable the Eleusinian. Dionysius, Bacchus, Orisis, Adonis, Thamuz, Apollo, &c., were names adopted in various languages, and in several countries, to designate the Divinity, who was the object of those ceremonies, and it is generally admitted that the sun was meant by these several denominations. [1]

Let us begin with a fact, not disputed, that in these ceremonies, a death and resurrection was represented, and that the interval between death and resurrection was sometimes three days, sometimes fifteen days.

Now, by the concurrent testimony of all ancient authors [2] the deities called Osiris, Adonis, Bacchus, &c. were names given to, or types, representing the sun,

---

[1] The number of authorities to prove this are collected in Kirker, vol. I p. 288.
Ogygia me Bacchum canit,
Osiris Egyptus putat,
Arabiæ gens Adoneum.
Ausonius in Myobarbum
[2] Meursius has collected all the authorities and fragments found in ancient authors upon the Eleusinian ceremonies.

considered in different situations, and contemplated under various points of view. [3]

Therefore, these symbolic representations, which described the sun as dead, that is to say, hidden for three days under the horizon, must have originated in a climate, where the sun, when in the lower hemisphere, is, at a certain season of the year, concealed for three days from the view of the inhabitants.

Such climate is, in fact, to be found as far north as latitude 66°, and it is reasonable to conclude, that, from a people living near the polar circle, the worship of the sun, with such ceremonies, must have originated; and some have supposed that this people were the Atlantides. [4]

The worship of the sun is generally traced to Mitraic rites, and those invented by the Magi of Persia. But if the sun could be made an object of veneration, if the preservation of fire could be thought deserving of religious ceremonies, it is more natural that it should be with a people living in a frozen clime, to whom the sun is the greatest comfort, whose absence under the horizon for three days is a deplorable event, and whose appearance above the horizon a real source of joy.

Not so in Persia, where the sun is never hidden for three days together under the horizon, and where its piercing rays are so far from being a source of pleasure, that to be screened from them, to enjoy cool shades, is one of those comforts, to obtain which all the ingenuity of art is exerted. The worship, therefore, of the sun, and the keeping sacred fires, must have been a foreign introduction into Persia.

The conjecture is strengthened by some important facts, which, referring to astronomical, allusions, place the scene out of Persia, though the theory is found there.

---

[3] Plutarchus, De Iside et Osiride.
[4] Recherches sur les Atlantides.

In the Boun Dehesch (translated by Anquetil Du Perron page 400) we find, that "the longest day of the summer is equal to the two shortest of the winter; and that the longest night in the winter is equal to the two shortest nights in summer."

This circumstance can only take place at the latitude of 49° 20', where the longest day of the year is of sixteen hours ten minutes, and the shortest of eight hours five minutes.

This latitude is far beyond the limits of Persia, where history places Zoroaster, to whom the sacred doctrines; of the Persian book Boun Dehesch are attributed. This proportion, then, of days and nights, as a general rule could only be true in Scythia, whether at the sources of the Irtisch, the Oby, the Jenisci, or the Slinger.

We know nothing of the antient history of those Scythians or Massagetes, but we know that they disputed their antiquity with the Egyptians,[5] and that the above principle, though attributed to the Persian Zoroaster, is only applicable to the country of those Scythians.

But let the origin of the mysteries of the sun begin where it may, they were celebrated in Greece, in various places, amongst others, at Appollonia, a city dedicated to Apollo, and situated in latitude 41° 22'.[6] In this latitude the longest day has fifteen hours, differing three hours from the length of the day when the sun is on the equinoxial: the reverse is the case with the nights.

This circumstance will account for the preservation of three days in these mysteries, even when celebrated in Greece, and also for the fifteen days, or representation of the number of fifteen in some of the Eleusinian rites.

The mysterious numbers were employed to designate such and similar operations of nature, for it is said that the

---

[5] Herodotus.
[6] Martiniere Dicc. Geogr. art. Appollonia.

Pythagorean symbols and secrets were borrowed from the Orphic or Eleusinian rites; and that they consisted in the study of the sciences and useful arts, united with theology and ethics, and were communicated in cyphers and symbols. [7] Similar intimations, as to the mystic import of numbers are found in many other authors. [8]

The letters, representing numbers formed cabalistic names, expressive of the essential qualities of those things they meant to represent; and even the Greeks, when they translated foreign names, whose cabalistic import they knew, so they rendered them by Greek letters, as to preserve the same interpretation in numbers, which we find exemplified in the name Nile. [9]

---

[7] Jamablicus. part. I cap. 32.

[8] Plutarchus (in vitæ Numæ) says, that "to offer an odd number to the celestial gods, and an even one to the terrestrial, is proper. The sense of which precept is hidden from the vulgar."
The same Plutarchus (in vitæ Lycurgi) explaining the number of the Spartan Senators, who were 28, says, "something perhaps there is in being a perfect number formed of seven, multiplied by four, and withal the first number after six that is equal to all its parts."
Another proof of the mystic import of numbers is found in Plutarchus (in vitæ Fabii.) "The perfection of the number three consists in being the first of odd numbers, the first of plurals, and containing in itself the first differences, and the first elements of all numbers."

[9] The fertility caused by the inundations of the Nile over the adjacent country caused this river to be considered as a mystic representation of the sun, parent of all fecundity of the earth; and therefore a name was given to it containing the number 365, or days in the solar year. The Greeks thus preserved the name.

N {Greek N}	50
E {Greek E}	5
I {Greek I}	10
Λ {Greek L}	30

But in the number three to which so many mystical and moral allusions were made, had a reference to the three celestial circles, two of which the sun touches, passing over the third in its annual course. [10]

The mysteries of Eleusis, the same as those of Dionysius or Bacchus, were supposed by some to have been introduced into Greece by Orpheus: [11] they may have come there from Egypt, but Egypt may have received them at a previous period from the Persians, and these again from the Scythians; but taking them only as we find them in Greece, we will give here an outline of their ceremonies.

The aspirant for these mysteries was not admitted a candidate till he had arrived at a certain age, and particular persons were appointed to examine and prepare him for the rites of initiation.[12] Those, whose conduct was found irregular, or who had been guilty of attrocious crimes, were rejected, those found worthy of admittance were then

---

O {Greek O}	70
Σ {Greek S}	<u>200</u>
	365

[10] Potter's Grec. Antiq.

[11] Dionysius Siculus, Lib. VI. says, that the Athenians invented the Eleusinian mysteries; but in the first book of his Library he says they were brought from Egypt by Erecteus.
Theodoret Lib. Grec. Affect, says, that it was Orpheus who invented those mysteries, imitating, however, the Egyptian festivities of Isis.
Arnobius and Lactantius describe those mysteries, as also does Clemens.

[12] Hesichius in γδραυ {Greek gdrau}
"They were exhorted to direct their passions. Porphir. ap. Sob. Ecclog. Phis. p. 142.
To merit promotion by improving their minds. Arrian in Epictet. lib. 3 cap. 21.

instructed by significant symbols in the principles of society. [13]

At the ceremony of admission into these mysteries, the candidate was first shown into a dark room, called the mystical chapel. [14] There certain questions were put to him. When introduced, the holy book was brought forward, from between two pillars or stones: [15] he was rewarded by the vision: [16] a multitude of extraordinary lights were presented to him, some of which are worthy of particular remark.

He stood on a sheep skin; the person opposite was called the revealer of sacred things [17] and he was also clothed in a sheep skin or with a veil of purple, and on his right shoulder a mule skin spotted or variegated, representing the rays of the sun and stars. [18] At a certain

---

[13] Clemens, Strom. Lib. I. p. 325. Lib. VIII. p. 854.

[14] μυςχος σηχος {Greek muṣxos shxoṣ}

[15] πετρωμα {Greek petrwma}

[16] αντοψια {Greek antopsia}

[17] ιεροφαντες {Greek ierofanteṣ}

[18] Mairobius Saturnalia. Lib. I. c. 8. I will copy here an English translation of this passage, which I have read some where.
"He who desires in pomp of sacred dress,
The Sun's resplendent body to express, p. 11
Should first a veil assume of purple bright.
Like fair white beams combined with fiery light;
On his right shoulder next, a mule's broad hide,
Widely diversified with spotted pride,
Should hang an image of the pole divine,
And doedal stars whose orbs eternal shine;
A golden splendid zone then, oe'r his vest
He next should throw, and bind it round his breast,
In mighty token how with golden light,
The rising sun from earth's last bounds, and night
Sudden emerges and with matchless force,
Darts through old Ocean's billows in his course,
A boundless splendour hence enshrined in dew,
Plays on his whirlpools, glorious to the view,
While his circumfluent waters spread abroad,
Full in the presence of the radiant god;

distance stood the torch-bearer, [19] who represented the sun; and beside the altar was a third person, who represented the moon. [20]

Thus we preceive, that over those assemblies presided three persons, in different employments, and we may remark, that in the government of the caravans in the eastern countries, three persons also direct them, though there are five principal officers, besides the three mathematicians; those three persons are, the commander in chief, who rules all; the captain of the march, who has the ruling power, as long as the caravan moves; and the captain of the rest, or refreshment, who assumes the government, as soon as the caravan stops to refresh. [21]

Some authors have observed the same division of power, in the march of the Israelites through the wilderness, and consider Moses as the captain general, Joshua the captain of the march; and perhaps Aaron as the captain of the rest. [22]

The society of which we are speaking, was ruled by three persons, with different duties assigned to them, by a custom of the most remote antiquity.

The mysteries, however, were not communicated at once, but by gradations, [23] in three different parts. The business of the initiation, properly speaking was divided

---

But Ocean's circle, like a zone of light,
The sun's wide bosom girds and charms the wand'ring sight.

[19] δαδουχοσ {Greek *dadouxos*}

[20] Atheneus, Lib. V. cap. 7. Apuleius. Lib. II. Metamorph.

[21] Fragments, added to Calmet's Dict.
Dissertation on the Caravans, taken from Col. Campbell's Travels in India.

[22] Ib.

[23] "The *perfective* part precedes initiation, and initiation precedes *inspection*." Proculs. in Theol. Plat. lib. IV. p. 220.

into five sections, as we find in a passage of Theo, who compares philosophy to those mystic rites. [24]

These ceremonies, thus far, appear to contain the lesser mysteries, or the first and second stages of the candidate in his progress through the course of his initiations. There was, however, a third stage, when the candidate, himself, was made symbolically to approach death, and then return to life. [25]

In this third stage of the ceremony, the candidate was stretched upon the couch,[26] to represent his death.

As to the festivities, in which those mysteries were celebrated, we find that on the 17th of the month Athyr [27]

---

[24] Again philosophy may be called the initiation into the sacred ceremonies, and the tradition of genuine mysteries; for there are five parts of initiation. The first is previous purgation; for neither are the mysteries communicated to all, who are willing to receive them; but there are certain characters, who are prevented by the voice of the crier; such as those who possess impure hands, and an inarticulate voice; since it is necessary that such as are not expelled from the mysteries should first be refined by certain purgations; but after purgation, the tradition of the sacred rights succeeds. The third part is denominated inspection. And the fourth, which is the end, fixing of the crowns: so that the initiated may, by these means, be enabled to communicate to others the sacred rites, in which he has been instructed; whether after this he become the torch-bearer, or an interpreter of the mysteries, or sustain some other part of the sacerdotal office. But the fifth, which is produced from all these, is friendship with divinity, and the enjoyment of that felicity, which arises from intimate converse with the gods. Theo of Smyrna, in Mathemat. p. 18.

[25] "I approached the confines of death, and treading on the threshold of Proserpine, and being carried through all the elements, I came back again to my pristine situation. In the depths of midnight I saw the sun glittering with a splendid light, together with the infernal and supernatural gods, and approaching nearer to those divinities, I paid the tribute of devout adoration."
Apuleius Metamorph. lib. III.

[26] παϛος {Greek pasos}

[27] This month Athyr, according to the Julian year answers to November, or the winter solstice; but with the Jews, the month of Thamuz, when the solemnities of Adonis were celebrated in Judea, was

the images of Osiris were enclosed in a coffin or ark: on the 18th was the search;[28] and on the 19th was the finding. [29]

Thug in fables or symbolical histories, relating to these mysteries, we find Adonis slain and resuscitated; the Syrian women weeping for Thamuz, &c.

Let us now examine what was meant by this symbolical death and resurrection, or by certain personages, said to have visited the Hades, and returning up again. [30]

---

in June, or summer solstice. The reason appears to be, that the Jews taking this month from the vague year of the Egyptians (and not from the fixed year) settled Thamuz in the summer solstice.
Selden. De diis Syriis.
Kirker, vol. I. p. 291.

[28] ζητησις {Greek zhthsis} Plutarchus.

[29] ευρεσις {Greek euresis} Plutarchus.

[30] We must here observe that the fables were intended to convey more than one meaning; in proof of which we copy the following passage: "Of fables some are theological, others animastical (or relating to the soul) others material, and lastly others mixed of all these. Fables are theological, which employ nothing corporeal, but speculate the very essence of the gods: such as the fable, which asserts, that Saturn devoured his children: for it insinuates nothing more than the nature of an intellectual god, since every intellect returns to itself. But we speculate fables physically when we speak concerning the energies of the gods about the world; as, when considering Saturn the same as time, and calling the parts of time the children of the universe, we assert that the children are devoured by their parent. But we employ fables in an animastic mode, when we contemplate the energies of the soul; because, the intellection of our souls, though by a discursive energy, they run into other things, yet abiding their parents. Lastly, fables are material, such as the Egyptians ignorantly employ, considering and calling corporeal natures divinities; such as Isis, Earth, Osiris, Humidity, Typhon, Heat; or again, denominating Saturn water, Adonis fruits, and Bacchus, wine. And, indeed, to assert that these are dedicated to the gods, in the same manner as herbs, stones, and animals, is the part of wise men; but to call them gods is alone the province of fools and madmen; unless we speak in the same manner, as when from established custom we call the orb of the sun and its rays the sun itself. But we may perceive the mixt kind of fables, as well in

It appears that this type in all its various forms and denominations, indicated the sun passing to the lower hemisphere, and coming again to the upper. [31]

The Egyptians, who observed this worship of the sun, under the name of Osiris, represented the sun in the figure of an old man, just before the winter solstice, and typified him by Serapis, having the constellation of Leo opposite to him, the Serpent or Hydra under him, the Wolf on the east of the Lion, and the Dog on the west. This is the state of the southern hemisphere at midnight about that period of the year.

The same Egyptians represented the sun by the boy Harpocrates, at the vernal equinox; and then was the festivity of the death, burial, and resurrection of Osiris; that is to say, the sun in the lower hemisphere; just coming up, and rising above in the upper hemisphere.

In this upper situation the sun was called Horus, Mithras, &c. and hailed as *sol invictus*. We will now point out some other symbols to express the same phenomena,

---

many other particulars, as when they relate, that discord, at the banquet of the gods through a golden apple, and that a dispute about it arising amongst the goddesses, they were sent by Jupiter to take the judgment of Paris, who, charmed with the beauty of Venus, gave her the apple in preference to the rest. For in this fable, the banquet denotes the supermundane powers of the gods, and on this account, a subsisting conjunction with each other: but the golden apple denotes the world, which on account of its composition from contrary natures, is not improperly said to be thrown by discord or strife. But again, since different gifts are imparted to the world by different gods, they appear to contest with each other for the apple. And a soul living according to sense, (for this is Paris) and not perceiving other powers in the universe, asserts that the apple is alone the beauty of Venus. Of these species of fables, such as are theological belong to philosophers, the physical and animastical to poets. But they were mixt with iniatiatory rites, and the intention of all mystic ceremonies is to conjoin us with the world and the gods."
Salust, the Platonic Philosopher.
[31] Orpheus, Hymn. Sol and Adon.

though different from those types we are treating of at present.

In the Mithraical astronomical monuments, where the figure of a man is represented conquering and killing a bull, there are two figures by their sides with torches; one pointing downwards, the other, upwards.

These monuments, where the mysteries in question were depicted, the man killing and conquering the bull, represent the sun, passing to the upper hemisphere, through the sign of Taurus, which in that remote period (four thousand six hundred years before our era) was the equinoxal sign. The two torch-bearers, the one pointing his torch downwards, the other upwards, represent the sun passing down to the lower hemisphere, and coming up again. [32]

At the remote time before alluded to, the sun entered the sign Taurus, at the summer equinox, and the year was begun at this period among the Egyptian astronomers. [33] Afterwards, in consequence of the precession of the equinoxes, the summer equinox took place in the sign of Aries; hence part of the Egyptians transferred their worship from the bull or calf to the ram; [34] while others continued to worship the bull. [35]

We may explain this in the language of our modern astronomers by saying, that some of the learned Egyptians

---

[32] Kirker, Vol. I. p. 217. Vide Hide, Hist. vet. Persar. 113.

[33] "The Egyptians began to reckon their months from the time when the sun enters, now, in the beginning of the sign Aries."
Rabb. A. Seba.

[34] Why has he (Aratus) taken the commencement of the year from Cancer, when the Egyptians date the beginning from Aries?"
Theon. p. 69.
Herodotus (L. 2. cap. 24) says, that the statue of Jupiter Ammon had the head of a ram, Eusebius (Præparat. Evang. L. 3. cap. 12.) tells us, that the idol Ammon had a ram's head with the horns of a goat.

[35] Strabo (L. 17.) informs us, that in his time, the Egyptians nowhere sacrificed sheep but in the Niotic Nome.

continued to reckon by the moveable zodiac, while others reckoned the year by the fixed zodiac; and this circumstance produced a division of sects in the people, as it was a division of opinion, amongst the learned.

Likewise, by the same precession of the equinoxes, the sun passed from Aries to Pisces in the vernal equinox, about three hundred and thirty eight years before our era; yet the beginning of the year continued to be reckoned from Aries. If the Egyptian astronomy and Egyptian religion had then existed with the same vigour, both would have perhaps suffered a similar alteration; but the Egyptian systems were at that period nearly annihilated. We may observe, however, that the Christians, at the beginning of our era, marked their tombs; with fishes, as an emblem of Christianity, to distinguish their sepulchers from those of the heathens, by a symbol unknown to them.

Returning from this short digression to our immediate purpose, we have to observe, that if those ceremonies and symbols were meant to represent the sun, and the laws of its motions, these very phenomena of nature were studied with a moral view, as being themselves types or arguments to a more sublime or metaphysical philosophy; and the moral rules therefrom deducted, were impressed on the memory by those lively images and representations.

The emerging of the sun into the lower hemisphere, and its returning, was contemplated either as a proof or as a symbol of the immortality of the soul; one of the most important, as well as the most sublime tenets of the Platonic Philosophy. [36]

---

[36] "Also Pindar, speaking of the Eleusinian mysteries, deducts this inference: "Blessed is he, who having seen the common things under the earth, also knows what is the end of life, for he knows the empire of Jupiter."
Clemens Strom. Lib. III. p. 518.
"Since in Phædo he venerates with a becoming silence, the assertion delivered in the Arcane Discourses; that men are placed in the body, as

The doctrines of the spirituality and immortality of the soul, explained by those symbols, were very little understood, even by the initiated; thus we find some of them [37] took those types to signify merely the present body, by their descriptions of the infernal abodes; whereas, the true meaning of these mysteries inculcated the doctrine of a future state of the soul, and future rewards and punishments; and that such were the doctrines of those philosophers is shown by many and indisputable authorities. [38]

The union of the soul with the body was considered as the death of the soul; its; separation as the resurrection of the soul; [39] and such ceremonies and types were intended to impress the doctrine of the immersion of the soul into matter as is well attested. [40]

---

in a certain prison, secured by a guard, and testifies, according to the mystic ceremonies, the different allotments of pure and impure souls in Hades; their habits, and the triple path p. 18 arising from their essences, and thus, according to paternal and sacred institutions, all which are full of symbolical theory, and of the poetical descriptions concerning the ascent and descent of souls, of Dionysial signs, the punishment of the Titans, the trivia and wanderings in Hades, and every thing of the same kind."

Proclus, in Comm. of Plauto's Politics, p. 723.

[37] Macrobius.

[38] "We live their death, and we die their life."
Macrobius himself.

[39] "The ancient Theologists also testify, that the soul is in the body, as it were in a sepulchre, to suffer punishment."
Clemens, Strom. Lib. III. p. 518.

[40] "When the soul has descended into generation she participates of evil, and profoundly rushes into the region of dissimilitude, to be entirely merged in nothing more than into dark mire."
Again,
"The soul therefore dies through vice, as much as it is possible for the soul to die, and the death of the soul is, while merged or baptized, as it were, in the present body, to descend into matter, and be filled with its impurity; and after departing from this body, to lie absorbed in its filth, till it returns to a superior condition, and elevates its eye from the

By the emblem of the sun descending into the lower hemisphere was also represented the soul of the man, who through ignorance and uncultivation, was in a state compared to sleep, or almost dead; which mystery was intended to stimulate man to the learning of sciences.[41]

The Egyptians also considered matter as a species of mud or mire, in which the soul was immerged;[42] and in an ancient author we find a recapitulation of these theories in the same sense.[43]

---

overwhelming mire. For to he plunged in matter is to descend into the Hades, and there fall asleep."
Plotinus, in Enead. I. Lib. VIII. p. 80.
"O wretched man that I am! who shall deliver me from the body of this death?"
Rom. VII. v. 24.

[41] He who is not able, by the exercise of his reason to define the idea of the good, separating it from all other objects, and piercing, as in a battle, through every kind of argument; endeavouring to confute, not according to opinion, but according to essence, and proceeding through all these dialetical energies, with an unshaken reason: he who cannot accomplish this, would you not say that he neither knows the good itself, nor any thing which is properly denominated good? And would you not assert that such a one, when he apprehends any certain image of reality, apprehends it rather through the medium of opinion than of science; that in the present life he is sunk in sleep, and conversant with delusions of dreams, and that before he is roused to a vigilant state, he will descend to Hades, and be overwhelmed with sleep perfectly profound?"
Plato, De Rep. Lib. VII.

[42] The Egyptians called matter (which they symbolically denominated water) the dregs or sediment of the first life, matter being, as it were, a certain mire or mud.
Simplicius, in Arist. Phis. p. 50.

[43] Lastly, that I may comprehend the opinion of the ancient theologists on the state of the soul after death, in a few words, they considered, as we have elsewhere asserted, things divine as the only realities, and that all others were only the images or shadows of truth. Hence they asserted that prudent men, who earnestly employed themselves in divine concerns, were above all others in a vigilant state. But that imprudent men, who pursued objects of a different nature, being laid

The Persians, who followed the tenets of Zerdoust, called by the Greeks Zoroaster, having received the same doctrines upon the mystical contemplation of the sun, made also the same metaphysical application to the soul, of the passage of the sun through the signs; of the zodiac.[44]

The sun, moreover, was considered as the symbol of the active principle; whereas the moon and earth were symbols of the passive.[45]

The sun itself, considering its beneficial influence in the physical world, was chosen as; the symbol of the Deity, though afterwards taken by the vulgar as a Deity.[46]

---

asleep, as it were, were only engaged in the delusions of a dream; and that if they happened to die in this sleep, before they were roused, they would be afflicted with similar and still sharper visions in a future state. And that he who in this life pursued realities, would, after death, enjoy the highest truth; so he who was conversant with fallacies, would hereafter be tormented with fallacies and delusions in the extreme: as the one would be delighted with true objects of enjoyment, so the other would be tormented with delusive semblances of reality."
Ficinus, De Immortalitate Anim.
Lib. XVIII. p. 411.

[44] Plato mentions, that this Zoroaster twelve days after his death, when already placed on the pile, came again to life, which perhaps represented, if not something more abstruse, the resurrection of those who are received in heaven, going through the twelve signs of the Zodiac; and he says, likewise, that they hold the soul to descend through the same signs when the generation takes place. This is to be taken in no other way, than the twelve labours of Hercules, by which, when done, the soul is liberated from all the pains of this world.
Clemens, Strom. Lib. V. p. 711.

[45] Apuleius.

[46] Mocopulus, in Hesoid, Ptol. See Cudworth, Book. I. chap. 4.
"This God, whether he ought to be called that which is above mind and understanding, or the idea of all things, or the one, (since unity seems to be the oldest of all things) or else, as Plato was wont to call him, the God, I say this uniform cause of all things, which is the origin of all beauty and perfection, unity and power, produced from himself a certain intelligible sun, every way like himself, of which the sensible sun is but an image."
Julian's Orat. in praise of the Sun.

It must be here particularly observed, that the different names, which the Egyptians (from whom the Greeks learnt them) gave to God, instead of meaning several gods were only expressions of the different productive effects of the only one God. [47] Not very different from what the Jews derive from the great name Tetragramaton. [48]

The fables, allegories, and types of the ancients, being of three classes, import some times various meanings;

"We see the unity (of God) as the sun from a distance obscurely, if you go nearer, more obscure still; and, lastly, it prevents seeing any thing else. Truly it is an incomprehensible light, inaccessible; and profoundly it is compared to the sun, to which the more you look the more blind you become."
Damascius, Platonicus, De Unitate.
The remains of the sectarians of Zoroaster, called now in Persia, Guebres, and who lead a miserable life, and more persecuted by the Mahomedans than the Jews are in Europe by the Christians, still perform their devotions, and say their prayers towards the sun or fire; but assert, that they do not adore them, only conceive them symbols of the Deity.
Vide Stanley, De Vet. Persar.
[47] "The first God, before the being and only, is the father of the first God, who he generated, preserving his solitary unity, and this is above the understanding, and that prototype which is said his own father his son, one father, and truly good God . . . . This is the beginning, God of gods, unity from one, above essence, the principle of essence, essence comes from him, for this reason is called father of essence: this is the being, the principle of intelligence; these are principles the most ancient of all . . . . . . This intelligence acting or operating, which is the truth of the Lord, and the science, in as much as it proceeds in generating, bringing to light the occult power of the concealed reasons, is called in the Egyptian language Ammon; but in as much as it acts without fallacy, and likewise artificially with truth, is called *Phta*; the Greeks call it Vulcan, considering the acting or operating; in as much as he is the operator of all good, is called Osiris, who in consequence of his superiority has many other denominations, in consequence of the many powers and different actions, which he exercises."
Jamblicus, De Myster. Egypt.
[48] The Hebrews call it שרופמה םש {Hebrew *ShM HMPWRSh*} Shem Hamphoresh.

19

therefore, some of the ceremonies to which sublime import is attached, are also applied to typify less dignified operations, in the natural system. Thus, for instance, the fable of Proserpine, which alludes to the immersion of the soul into the body, was also employed to symbolize the operation of the seed in the ground.[49]

But the general doctrine of Plato of the descent of the soul into the darkness; of the body, the perils of the passions, the torments of vices, appears to be perfectly described by Virgil;[50] though this Poet was of the Epicurean sect, the most fashionable in his days.

The lesser mysteries represented, as we have seen, the descent of the soul into the body, and the pains therein suffered. The greater mysteries were intended to typify the splendid visions, or the happy state of the soul, both here and hereafter, when purified from the defilements of material nature. These doctrines are also inculcated, by the fables of the fortunate islands, the Elysian fields, &c. The different purifications in these rites were symbols of the gradation of virtues, necessary to the re-ascent of the soul. Inward purity, of which external purifications were symbols, can only be obtained by the exercise of these virtues.[51]

---

[49] Porphyr. cited by Eusebius, De Præp. Lib. III. cap. 2.

[50] Eneid. Lib. VI.

[51] "In the sacred rites, popular purifications are in the first place brought forth, and after these those as are more Arcane. But in the third place, collections of various things into one are received; after which follows inspection. The ethical and political virtues, therefore, are analogous to the apparent (or popular) purifications. But such of the cathartic virtues as banish all external Impressions correspond to the more occult purifications. The theoretical energies about intelligibles are analogous to the collections; but the contraction of these energies into an indivisible nature, corresponds to initiation. And the simple self-inspection of simple forms, is analogous to epoptic vision." Olimpiodorus, in Plato's Phæd.

To the allusion of these virtues must be understood what Socrates says, that it is the business of the philosophers to study to die and to be themselves death; and as at the same time he reprobates suicide, such death cannot mean any other but philosophical death, or the exercise of what he calls the cathartic virtues.

If such was the meaning and import of the Eleusinian and Dionysian rites, symbols, and ceremonies, it must be allowed that a society or sect, which was employed in the contemplation of such sublime truths, cannot be looked upon as trifling or profligate.

The very Christian Fathers, who so strongly attacked the Pagan religion, confessed the utility of these symbols;[52] and that the circumstances previous to initiation into those mysteries, tended to exclude impious notions, and prepare the mind to hear the truth. [53]

Those mysteries were concealed from the vulgar; because it would be a ridiculous prostitution of such sublime theories to disclose them to the multitude incapable of understanding them, when even many of the initiates, for want of study and application, did not comprehend the whole meaning of the symbols.

The multitude were told only in the abstract, the doctrine of a future state of rewards and punishments, and were made acquainted with the calendar, the result of astronomical observations; the knowledge of which was connected with their festivities and agricultural pursuits.

---

[52] "The interpretation of the symbolic kind is useful in many respects; for it leads to theology, to piety, and to show the ingenuity of the mind, the conciseness of expression, and serves to demonstrate science." Clemens, Strom. Lib. V. p. 673.

[53] "For before the delivery of these mysteries, some expiations ought to take place, that those, who were to be initiated, should leave impious opinions, and be converted to the true tradition." Clemens, Strom. Lib. VII. p. 848.

They were likewise taught other practical parts of science calculated for general use.

The secrecy of these mysteries was the first cause of obloquy against them; next came, beyond doubt, the depravity of their followers, and the perversion of those assemblies into convivial meetings first, and then into the most debauched associations.

Secrecy, also, was enjoined by the laws, it was death to reveal any thing belonging to the Eleusinian mysteries; to disclose imprudently any thing about them, was supposed even indecorous; of this we find a very conspicuous; instance in Plutarch. [54]

Out of respect for this custom the scholars were, in general, only instructed in the *exoteric* doctrines. [55] The *acroamatic* doctrines were taught only to the few select, by private communication and *viva voce*.

Rut when the ignorance of the very teachers of those mysteries caused their forms only to be attended to, the essence was lost, the shadow only remained; and, then, even those forms and ceremonies were frequented by persons, ignorant of their import, and wicked enough to turn them to their private interests, as a machine employed

---

[54] "Alexander gained from him (Aristotle) not only moral and political knowledge, but was also instructed in those more secret and profound branches of science, which they call *epoptic* and *acroamatic*; and which they did not communicate to every common scholar. For when Alexander was in Asia, and received information that Aristotle had published some books, in which those points were discussed, he wrote to him a letter, in behalf of Philosophy, in which be blamed the course he had taken. The following is a copy of it."
"Alexander to Aristotle, prosperity.--You did wrong in publishing the acroamatic parts of science. In what shall we differ from others, if the sublimer knowledge, which we gained from you, be made common to all the world? For my part, I had rather excel the bulk of mankind in the superior parts of learning, than in the extent of power and dominion. Farewell."
Plutarch, in vit. Alex.
[55] Aulus Gellius. Lib. XX. cap. 5.

in deceiving the people, and to occasions of debauchery and depravity. We shall give an example of this,

The mysteries of Eleusis, or the Sun, were united or analogous to those of Dionysius or Bacchus; because, according to the Orphic theology, the intellect of every planet was denominated Bacchus: so when the sun was considered as the spiritual intelligence, who moved or caused this planet to move, in its annual circle, he was denominated Trietericus Bacchus. [56]

The ceremonies, therefore, of Bacchus, were attended with rejoicings, as the triumph of the spirit over matter; but this circumstance, so intimately connected with the sublime notions of the Eleusinian mysteries, was completely turned into a mere banqueting, and processions of drunken people, who of the ceremonies knew nothing else, than to carry branches of trees in their hands. [57]

More, still: a depraved priest introduced those Bacchanalian mysteries into Rome, for the very worst of purposes, which alarming the Senate, the most severe punishment was inflicted on him and his followers. [58]

In consequence of those abuses, it was, that Socrates refused to be initiated,[59] and the same did Diogenes, alledging that Pataecion, a notorious robber, had obtained initiation:[60] Epaminondas, also, and Agesilaus never desired it. [61]

---

[56] "He is called Dionysius, because he is carried with a circular motion through the immensely extended heavens."
Orphic vers. apud.

[57] "Indeed there are, as the saying is, many, who go into the mysteries: a multitude certainly of branch bearers (Thyrsirii) but very few Bacchians."
Socrates, in Plato; apud. Clemens Strom. Lib. I. p. 372.

[58] Livii. Lib. XXXIX. cap. 8 and 18.

[59] Lucian, in Demonat. tom. 2. p. 308.

[60] Plutarch. De aud. Poet. tom. 2. p. 21.

[61] Diogen. Laert. Lib. VI. § 39.

But if those who were desirous of being licentious clothed themselves with those mysteries, this has nothing to do with the original tenets of the institution. For the purity of its votaries was carried, according to the primitive mysteries, to the most delicate and scrupulous point.[62]

After such respectable authorities, as we have referred to, we must reject, as impudent calumnies, the assertion of Tertullian, who says, that the natural parts of a man were enclosed in the ark carried about in the processions of those mysteries: Theodoret and Arnobius say, they were the parts of a woman: such assertors had no means of ascertaining what was not known to any one, out of the precincts of those most recondite mysteries. [63]

---

[62] "A woman asked, how many days ought to pass, after she had congress with her husband, before she could attend the mysteries of Ceres. The answer was, with your husband immediately, with a strange man never."
Clemens, Strom. Lib. IV. p. 619.

[63] As a proof of the sublime ideas of God, entertained by the Egyptian sages, in contradiction to these gross accusations., we copy the following passages, from the very Mercurius Trimegistus, as related by Pimandrus.
"The Artificer fabricated the whole universe with his word, not with his hands. He however has it always present in his mind, acting all, one only God, constituting every thing with his will; this is his body, not tangible, not visible, nor similar to any other: for he is not fire, not waiter, not air, not even spirit; but from him depend every thing good; however, such he is, as every thing belongs to him."
Again,
"But that you should not want the principal name of God, nor you should be ignorant of what is clear, and seems concealed from many; for, if it never appears, it is nowhere. Whatever appears only to your sight is created; what is concealed is all eternal; nor is it a reason why it should appear, as it never ends; he puts every thing before our eyes, but he remains concealed; because he enjoys an all eternal life: clearly he brings every thing to light, but he delights in the *adytum*; one, and uncreated, incomprehensible to our imagination (phantasia); but as every thing is enlightened by him, he shines in all and through all

We should rather guess, that in the ark, carried in the procession, and said to enclose the body of Osiris, spheres were deposited, representing our solar system. [64]

In regard to these accusations, found in some of the ecclesiastical writers, we must also observe, that many of them, led by a mistaken zeal for the Christian religion, disfigured in a most reprehensible degree, the ancient historical monuments: taking, for instance, the manner in which the history of Egypt as written by Manethon, was transmitted to us by those ecclesiastical writers:[65] others; of

---

things; and yet appears chiefly to those, to whom he is pleased to communicate his name."
Again,
"There is nothing in nature that is not him; he is all that exists; he is even what is not; and what is, he brought into light. And as nothing can be made without a maker, so you must think that unless God is always acting, it is impossible for any thing to exist in heaven, air, earth, sea, in all the world, in any particle of the world, in what is as well as in what is not. This is with the best name, God; this, again, is the most powerful of all things; this, conspicuous in mind; this, present with eyes; this, incorporeal; this, as it were, multi-corporeal, for nothing is in the bodies that is not in him; because, he alone exists in all; he has all names; because be is the only father; so it has no name because he is the father of all."
Apud Kirker, Vol. II. p. 504.
[64] Synesius, speaking of the Egyptian hierophant; observes thus; "they have χωμαστη᾿ρια {Greek xwmasth᾿ria}, which are arks, concealing, they say, the spheres."
See Plutar. De Iside and Orsiride.
[65] Julius Africanus, a Christian Priest, by birth a Jew, made a short compendium of the history of Manethon, that the author himself might be dispensed with: this was about the year 230 of the Christian era. Finding that the Egyptian Chronology represented the world some thousands of years older than the chronology of the Bible, he so disfigured the dates of Manethon as to make him agree with the Bible. Moreover, this work of Africanus is also lost, and we have only extracts of it, preserved in the work of a monk, generally known by the name of Syncellus, who confesses that he mutilated and altered Africanus. Now this individual not even had the original Bible, but only the Greek translation, which avowedly has the chronology

such writers, in fact, knew nothing of the Egyptian mysteries. [66]

The conclusion, therefore, is, that the motives of those institutions were good and pure, as tending to the study of science, and practice of morality, though the same institutions afterwards degenerated;[67] and their

---

vitiated; and yet Manethon's data were to be disfigured and interpolated, to make it square with the incorrect Greek translation of the Bible.

[66] "Celsus seems to me, here, to do just as if a man, travelling into Egypt, where the wise men of the Egyptians, according to their country learning, philosophize much, about those things that are accounted by them divine, whilst the ideots, in the mean time, hearing only certain fables, which they know not the meaning of, are very much pleased therewith: Celsus, I say, does as if such sojourner in Egypt who had conversed only with those ideots, and not been at all instructed by any of the priests, in their arcane and recondite mysteries, should boast that he knew all that belonged to the Egyptian theology."
Origines, contra Celsum, Lib. I. p. 11.

"When amongst the Egyptians there is a king chosen out of the military order, be is forthwith brought to the priests, and by them instructed in that arcane theology which conceals mysterious truths under obscure fables and allegories."
Plutarch. De Iside, p. 354.

[67] We will content ourselves, here with the authority of Kircher, one of the most learned antiquarians in Egyptian matters.
"Therefore, Hermes, that great author of the hieroglyphic doctrine, elucidating many things, chiefly about God, and his perfections, also of the creation of the world, and its preservation, of the administration of the same world and its parts, both by himself, and through his angels, as he heard of the Patriarchs about the government of the world, endeavoured seriously to penetrate these things: hence sprang a new philosophy in which as he treated of more sublime things than the ignorant could understand, he veiled under a new art, afterwards called hieroglyphic, which was hidden from rude understandings, not in wooden monuments, but in mystic figures, engraved in hard stones, for an eternal memorial with posterity; as a sublime science of things deserving eternal veneration, and worthy of being recommended to all; and in imitation of the great eternal Artificer, in the administration of the world, he so constituted his system, that it was communicated only to the select hieromists, priests, stolists, and hierogramatists, men of

degeneration was followed by the ruin of the state, as predicted by Trimegistus himself, who in this prediction proved how great a philosopher and politician he was.[68]

Having thus established what was the meaning and import of the Eleusinian or Dionysian mysteries amongst the ancient Greeks, who transmitted to us the knowledge of them; and having shown that the ceremonies were not intended in their origin as a worship of the sun, considered as a Deity, we shall proceed to examine how those mysteries were communicated to other nations by the Greeks.

About fifty years[69] before the building of the Temple of Solomon in Jerusalem, a colony of Grecians, chiefly

---

great genius, wise for the government of the state, according to the rules of administration, prescribed in the obelisks, and men who had shown ability and aptitude, and were moreover restricted, by oath, to keep it secret. By these means the priests, being looked upon by all with admiration, in consequence of their science in those new things, expressed in the symbols, were honoured by the multitude almost as half gods. But to increase this veneration they told the people many things about the apparitions of the gods, their answers, and how they were to be worshipped to sooth them and make them propitious: to this we must add the great profit they had by their machines and mechanical inventions and their skill in mathematics; and their making statues that moved their eyes and head, to express approbation or disapprobation: and that the miserable multitude was deceived and beguiled, paying always to obtain a favor from the gods, or to avert their anger. Hence it came, that in the course of time, that religion conceived by Trimegistus in a sincere sense, was by degrees degenerated into open and declared idolatry."
Kircher, vol. IV. p. 82.

[68] "O Egypt, Egypt, of thy religion only the fables remain, and those incredible to thy posterity."
Trimegistus, in Asclepio.

[69] The emigration of the Ionians to Asia Minor is mentioned by Herodotus, and others, but the epoch is fixed by various authors differently:

Ionians, complaining of the narrow limits of their country, in an increased population, emigrated; and having been settled in Asia Minor, gave to that country the name of Ionia. [70]

No doubt that people carried with them their manners, sciences, and religion; and the mysteries of Eleusis [71] among the rest. Accordingly we find that one of their cities, Byblos, was famed for the worship of Apollo, as Apollonia had been with their ancestors. [72]

These Ionians, participating in the improved state of civilization in which their mother country, Greece, then was, cultivated the sciences, and useful arts; but made

By Playfair in the year B. C	1044
Gillies	1055
Barthelemy. Anacharsis	1076

[70] "It is said, that the chief of the Ionian colony was Androclus, a legitimate son of Codrus, the king of Athens; so it is related, that the Ionians established their royalty; and those descending from that race, even now, are called kings, and enjoy their boners, that is to say, a place where they attend the spectacles and the public games, wearing the royal purple, and a staff instead of the sceptre, and the Eleusinian rites."
Strabo, Lib. XIV. p. 907.
This emigration is also mentioned by Herodotus, Lib. I. cap. 142, and 148; Aelianus, Lib. VIII. Pausanias, in Achaicis; Plutarchus, in Homero, Veleius Paterculus, in Chronico. Clemens, Lib. I. Strom.
[71] Vide Strabo, above.
[72] "Byblos was capital of Cinera, and there was a temple of Apollo, situated on an elevated spot, not far from the sea. Afterwards is the river called Adonis."
Strabo, Lib. XVI. p. 1074.

28

themselves most conspicuous in architecture, and invented or improved the order called by their own name Ionian.

These Ionians formed a society, whose purpose was to employ themselves in erecting buildings. The general assembly of the society, was first held at Theos; but afterwards, in consequence of some civil commotions, passed to Lebedos. [73]

This sect or society was now called the Dionysian Artificers, as Bacchus was supposed to be the inventor of building theatres; and they performed the Dionysian festivities.[74] They afterwards extended themselves to Syria, Persia, and India.[75]

From this period, the Science of Astronomy which had given rise to the symbols of the Dionysian rites, became connected with types taken from the art of building.[76]

These Ionian societies divided themselves into different sections, or minor assemblies.[77] Some of those

---

[73] "Lebedos, was the seat and assembly of the Dionysian Artificers, who inhabit from Ionia to the Hellespont; there they had annually their solemn meetings and festivities in honor of Bacchus. Their first seat was Theo.
Strabo, Lib. XIV. p. 921.
The Latin translator of Strabo renders the Dionysian Artificers (Διονυσιος τεχνε {Greek *Dionusios_ texne*}) *scenicos artificers*; because Bacchus or Dionysus was supposed to be the inventor of theatres and *scena*, derived from the Heb. שכן {Hebrew *ShKZ*}, to inhabit.
[74] Polydor. Virg. de Rer. Invent, I. 3. c. 13.
[75] Strabo, p. 471.
[76] From the application of instruments of architectuure to morality, the Platonic and Pythagorean philosophers took not only types but words to explain our moral ideas.
For instance, a *right* man (rectus); *obligation*, from ligament (ligare) and from the same law (lex a ligare); to *square* our actions (quadrare) *Justum aequum*, &c. *Rude* mind, *polished* mind; from *rude* stone, and *polished* stone, &c.
[77] The meetings or assemblies of the Dionysian Artificers went by various names, (ας συνοιχια {Greek *as_ sunoixia*}) *contubernium*, which was the place of their meeting. The society was called

small or dependent associations; had also their distinguishing names. [78]

But they extended their moral views, in conjunction with the art of building, to many useful purposes, and to the practice of acts of benevolence. [79]

We find recorded, that these societies, and their utility, were many years afterwards inquired into, by Cambyses, king of Persia, who approved of them, and gave to them great marks of favour. [80]

---

sometimes συναγωγη {Greek *sunagwgh*} (*collegium*); ἅρεσις {Greek *á?resis*}; (*secta*); συνοδος {Greek *sunodos*} (*congregatio*) χοινος {Greek *xoinos*}; (*communitas*).

Aulus Gellius, Lib. cap. II.

[78] See Chiseul, Antiquitates Asiaticæ, p. 95.

[79] "This example imitated those Ionians who emigrated from Europe to the maritime countries of Caria (Asia Minor) and also the Dorians, their neighbours, building temples at a common expense. The Ionians built the temple of Diana at Ephesus, the Dorians that of Apollo at Triopii, where at a certain period they repaired with their wives and children, and there performed sacred rites, and had a market, likewise games, races, wrestlings, music-parties of different kinds, and made common offerings to the gods. When they had performed the spectacles and the business of the market, or fair, and fulfilled towards each other the duties of fellow creatures, if there was any litigation between the cities, they sat as judges to settle the dispute: moreover, in these assemblies they debated as to the war with the barbarians, and the means of keeping a mutual concord amongst the nations."

Dionis. Halicarn. Lib. III p. 229. edit. 1691.

[80] "After this, the inhabitants of Ionia thought proper to apply to Cambyses, and having represented to him what was their business, the king ordered them into his presence, and asked who they were, and how they came to live in his dominions; and having examined and ascertained from whence they proceeded, he admired them, and chose rather that they should be erected into a society by himself, than to allow that he received such as coming from another country; for he thought it was not decorous to receive favours from others, who sojourned in his country, as if he would receive those services as pay for their habitations; and, therefore, to show this, dismissed them with presents, as marks of his munificence."

Libanius in Orat. XI. Antiochus. Vol. II. p. 343.

It is essential to observe, that these societies; had significant words to distinguish their members;[81] and for the same purpose they used emblems taken from the art of building.[82]

Let us now notice the passage of the Dionysian Artificers to Judea. Solomon obtained from Hiram, king of Tyre, men skilful in the art of building, when the Temple was erected at Jerusalem.[83] Amongst the foreigners, who came on this occasion, we find men from Gabel, called Giblim;[84] that is to say, the Ionians settled in Asia Minor, for Gabbel, or Byblos, was that city where stood the temple of Apollo, where the Eleusinian rites or Dionysian mysteries were celebrated, as we have already stated.[85]

---

[81] Robertson's Greece, p. 127.

[82] Eusebius de Prep. Evang. L. III. c. 12. p. 117.

[83] I Kings, chap. v.

[84] The English translation of the Bible in I Kings c. v. v. 18 where the original Hebrew says Gibblim (םילבג {Hebrew *GBLYM*}) or Gibblites, which means inhabitants of Gebbel, renders it, by the appellative, stone squares. The proof that this reading is not correct, is not only because of the different opinions of all other translations, which understand by this Gibblim the inhabitants of Gebbel; but that the same English p. 34 translation, in another part of the Bible, renders the same word by the ancients of *Gebbal*. (Ezek. ch. xxvii. v. 9.)
Now that Gabbel was the same as Byblos is clear; because the Septuagint version always translates this Gebbel for Byblos, and though there were several cities of this name, yet this one seems to be that which is between Tripoli and Berite; and still called Gebail.
In fact, Lucian, in his Treatise De Dea Syria, says expressly, that Gabala was Byblos, famous for the worship of Adonis.

[85] For we find in Ezekiel these words "And I saw the women sitting weeping for Thamuz," that is to say, Adonis. Such, however, was what was done by the inhabitants of those cities, in testimony of which, they sent letters to women who were at Byblos, when Adonis was found, and afterwards scaled and thrown into the sea, they say they were spontaneously carried to Byblos; and, when arrived there, women ceased to weep for Adonis."
Procopius in Isaiah c. xviii.

We could, in addition to this argument produce some authority; for Josephus says that the Grecian style of architecture was used at the temple of Jerusalem. [86]

After this we cannot be surprised to find that the ceremonies of Eleusis, or Thamuz, should be introduced into Judea, particularly, as Solomon himself, after having entered into the scientific allusions, in the construction of the temple, was not free from the accusation of the gross superstition of idolatry. [87]

So we find some years afterwards the prophet Ezekiel complaining that the Israelitish women were weeping for Thamuz at a certain period of the year, at the very gates of the temple.[88]

But it is natural to suppose that the Dionysian Artificers would not have attempted to introduce those rites amongst the religious Jews, as a mere matter of idolatry, for the worship of the sun. The ideas of the Israelites, concerning the unity of God, would have revolted at any thing, inducing a belief of the polytheism of the Gentiles.

The symbol, therefore, in these mysteries, must have been explained to the Jews, to mean only the sun, in the true and original sense of those mysteries; that is to say, as

---

[86] Josephus Antiquit. Lib. VIII. c. 5.

[87] I Kings chap. xi. v. 5, and 6.

[88] Ezek. c. viii. v. 14. Thamuz signifies the name of a month, and likewise the name of an idol or divinity, which even in the opinion of St. Jerome is the same as Adonis. Plutarch says that the Egyptians called Osiris Ammuz, and from thence was corruptly derived the name of Jupiter Ammon. Robertson (Thesaurus Linguæ Sanctæ) says that the word Ammuz (read Ammoum) used by Herodotus and Plutarch, were corruptions from the Hebrew Thamuz (Hebrew תמוז {Hebrew *TMWZ*}). I would rather say that the word was originally Egyptian, and made Hebrew by the addition of the formative ת {Hebrew *T*}); and the more so, as Ammuz in the Egyptian language signifies (by the explanation of Manetho in Plutarch) something abstruse or concealed; which has an evident allusion to the concealment or symbolical death of Osiris or Adonis.

32

an emblem of God's goodness to man; and the apparent motions of that luminary, first as the guide for fixing the seasons; next as types or remembrances of the immortality of the soul: for this dogma does not appear either clear in the books of the Jews before that period, or universally admitted amongst them at a much later date. [89]

To avoid, therefore, any allusion to idolatry in these ceremonies and symbols, another personage or another name must have been substituted for Adonis or Osiris; and as a symbolical death and resurrection was essential, in the allegory of the system, the history of the death of another individual must have been substituted . . . . . .

However, in framing this new symbolical history, such circumstances were to be related, connected with the death of that personage, as to typify and account for the whole of the Eleusinian mysteries, or the passage of the sun from the upper to the lower hemisphere, and its return up again. [90]

In the formation of this new system, or rather new allegory to the same system, though the name of the hero was changed, the circumstances must have been preserved, as far as consistent with new names . . . .

The whole fabric of the temple would favor an allusion of this sort.

The foundation stone was laid on the second day of the second month;[91] which corresponds upon an average to the 20th of April; reckoning the sacred year, upon the fixed zodiac.

Now if you rectify your globe to the latitude of Jerusalem (31.° 30') at that period of the year, you will have

---

[89] Mark. chap. xii. v. 18.

[90] Thus in the numbers, 3, 5, 7, 12, 15 must have been preserved as essential. In the ceremonies, the symbol of death and resurrection; the crossing of the equinoxial twice, &c. In the time, the season of the year, when the sun arrives at the two tropics, the rising, the southing, the setting, &c.

[91] Chron. chap. iii. v. 2.

the sun in Aries, or the sun represented by a ram or sheep, or a man in a sheep's skin; as the hierophant was represented, in the mysteries of Eleusis.

Therefore, the very period of the year in which the foundation stone of the temple was laid, would afford an opportunity of establishing upon it a new allegorical system, to explain the ancient mystery.

If we suppose the globe to represent the world in the position above described, the aspirant being in the west facing the hierophant, who in the east represents; the rising sun, the candidate will find himself between the two tropics, represented by the two columns[92] which were placed on the west entrance of that temple . . . . . .

The better to understand the facility with which the ancient system could be adapted to the circumstances of the temple of Jerusalem, we must consider its typic emblems, according to the notions of the Jews, and some of the Christian fathers.

The temples built in honor of the several gods, were so shaped, as to have allusion to the supposed attributes of such gods.[93] But the universe was supposed by the Platonists to be the true temple of the true and only God.[94] The temple, therefore, dedicated to the true God, was to be a type of the universe.

Thus we find that the temple of Jerusalem was situated east and west, and with dimensions and types all adapted to represent the universal system of nature.[95]

---

[92] πετρωμα {Greek petrwma}

[93] Vitruvius Lib. IV. c. 5.

[94] "Justly, therefore, Plato knowing the world to be the temple of God, showed a place in the city where the symbols should answer."
Clemens, Strom. Lib. V. p. 691.

[95] We shall here first quote the authority of the Jews on this point.
"Now let us consider what may be subindicated by the cherubim and flaming sword turning every way. What if this ought to be thought the circumvolution of the whole heavens?"

"But of the flaming sword turning every way, it may thus be understood to signify the perpetual motion of these (Cherubim) and of the whole heavens. But what if it be taken otherwise? So that the two cherubim signify both hemispheres."
Philo Judeus, p. 111, & 112.

"The tunic of the high priest since it was of linen, represents the earth; but the blue, the pole of heaven; the lightenings were indicated by the pomegranates; the thunders by the sound of the bells, &c. . . . ."

". . . . But the two sardonixes, with which the pontifical garment is clasped, denotes the sun and the moon, but if any one wish to refer the twelve stones to the twelve months, or to the same number of stars (constellations) in the circle, which the Greeks called the zodiac, he will not wander from the true meaning."
Josephus, Antiq. Lib. III.

Now for the Christian Fathers:

"It would be too long to follow the prophetical and legal (statements) which have been expressed by enigmas: almost the whole of the divine Scripture offer up these sort of oracles.

"He who reasons properly will find sufficient for the purpose, we shall give a few examples. So for instance what the ancients told of the temple, the seven enclosures, which also refer to other things in the history of the Hebrews, and what was inside by the apparatus of divers Symbols, referring to appearances, signify in their composition what refers, to heaven and earth. They signify, then, what to the nature of the elements imports the revelation of God. For the purple comes from the water, the linen (Βυσοσ {Greek *Busos*}) from the earth, the blue (hyacinthus) from the colour of the sky, as it is dark; the scarlet, the fire. In the middle, however, of the Temple was the veil, beyond which only the priests could go; there was the censer, symbol of the earth, which is this world, and from which exaltations takes place. But that place, which afterwards inside of the veil, where only the high priest had permission to enter, and that on certain days; the external court which was open to all Hebrews, they say was the medium between heaven and earth. Others say it was the symbol of the world, which is perceived by our intellectual senses. But the opening which separated the infidelity of the people, was extended before five columns, and separated those who were in the court."
Clemens, Strom. L. V. p. 665.

This Christian Father explains these columns, by the following passage of Plato:

"Plato says we must contemplate these columns, and diligently see that no profane person dares to go there. Those are profane who believe that

35

If the temple of Solomon was a type of the universe, to symbolize that Jehovah was no local God, but the only God, Lord of the universe; tradition also tells us that the place of assembly of the Dionysian Artificers was allegorically described by its dimensions, as a symbol of the universe, in length, in breadth, in height, and in depth.

---

nothing exists, but what they can touch with their hands, but the actions and generations, and all those things, which we cannot see, in things which exist, are without number. Such are those who attend to nothing else beyond the five senses."

Clemens, Strom. Lib. V. "Now for the candlestick, which was placed on the south of the censer. By this was exemplified the motion of the seven planets, which have their motions in the south. For on each side of the candlestick were branches, and in them lamps; because, the sun also, as a lamp, is placed in the middle of the other errant (stars), and those which are above it, and those which are below it, by a certain divine harmony receive light from him."

Clemens, Strom. Lib. V. p. 666.

"Those things, however, told of the sacred ark, signify the world as perceived by the intellectual senses, which are occult and shut to the vulgar. Besides those golden images, each having six wings, they either signify the two bears, as some will have it; or, what seems more convenient, the two hemispheres. Indeed the name of cherubim signifies an extensive knowledge. But both have two wings, and thus signify the sensible world, and the time carried on by the circle of the zodiac."

Clemens, Strom. Lib. V. p. 667.

"But the 360 bells, pending from the long robe (of the priest) are the times of the year; for it is said, this is the year of the Lord, preaching and sounding the great arrival of the Saviour."

Clemens, Strom. Lib. V. p. 668.

"The two brilliant emerald stones, which are on the shoulder-piece, signify the sun and the moon, which are the helpers of nature. For is was supposed the shoulder to be the beginning of the hand. But those other twelve stones, which are disposed in four rows, describe to us the circle of the zodiac, and agreeing to the four seasons of the year."

Clemens, Strom. Lib. V. p. 691.

The ancients represented the course of the stars, by the winding of a snake; but if this snake was so placed as to have the tail in her mouth, it then represented eternity.

Now if we consider the beginning of the civil year amongst the Hebrews, the month Tisri, which was in the winter equinox;[96] the sun, proceeding from thence, approaches the south, and touches the tropic of Capricorn; then retrocedes towards the north, crossing the equinoxal, and touching the tropic of Cancer; from whence retroceding again to the south, arrives at the equinoxial, finishing the year.

These points, in an extended map of the two hemispheres seem separate; but the emblem of the snake biting its tail, would represent the end of the year, meeting the beginning. [97]

---

[96] The first civil month of the Jews, called Tisri, (ירשית {Hebrew TYShRY}) was from the Egyptain Misri, changing only the formative ט {Hebrew T̲} into ת {Hebrew T}. And the word was derived from רמי {Hebrew YMR} (*rectum esse*), as then the sun was in the equinoxial: and the Rabbins, to this day, call the equinoxial ירשים {Hebrew MYShRY}. The Greeks spelling badly the name called this Egyptian month ημυϛορυ {Greek hmus̲oru}.

[97] The number 12, which is that of the months of the year, and alluded to in so many types of the Temple, must have afforded also facilities to establish the system of the Dionysian Artificers; and therefore we shall give some idea of the heathen philosophy attached to this number, in the following extracts from Suidas:

"The great Demiurgos, or architect of the universe, employed twelve thousand years, in the work he has produced, and divided in twelve times the twelve houses of the sun."

Suidas, Art. Tyrrhenia.

"In the first thousand, he made the heaven and earth. In the second thousand, the firmament (expansion) which he called coelum. In the third thousand, he made the sea, and the water that runs on the earth. In the fourth, he made two great torches of nature. In the fifth, he made the quadrupeds, animals that live on the earth and in the waters. In the sixth, he made the man."

"The first six thousand years having preceded the formation of the human race, it seems it will not exist but during six thousand years,

which are the others to complete the period of twelve thousand, at the end of which the world will finish."
Suidas Ib.
Now if you take each sign of the zodiac for 24,000 years, you will explain the above mystery. When the sun comes out of Aries, or the spring sign, the world is said to be born; here the period of life begins. When the sun is in Cancer, or the summer, is the pleasure and delights of life. When in Libra, life has declined: after that all is winter of death; and from this arise the fables about the four ages of the world.
The books of the Persian Mythology explain to us the same meaning.
"Time is 12,000 years, it is said in the law, that the celestial people were three thousand years to exist, and then the enemy (Satan or Arhiman) was not in the world, which makes six thousand years . . . ."
"The thousand of good appeared in the Lamb, the Bull, the Taurus, the Cancer, the Lion, and the Sheep, which make six thousand years. After the thousand of God, comes the Scale (Libra), Arhiman came into the world (that is to say the winter)."
Boun Dehesh; translation du Perron, p. 420.
"Orsmud, speaking in the law, says, 'I made the productions of the world in 365 days:' it is for this reason that the six *gahs gahambars* (months) are included in the year."
ib. p. 400.
Astronomically speaking, there is no period or cycle of 12,000 years. But Dupuis has solved the mystery, by saying, that the periods of the ancient Indians and Chaldeans, answered to the series 1, 2, 3, 4, or 4, 3, 2, 1.
Thus the duration of the four ages of the world, according to the Ezour Vedan, were

1st age	4,000	years
2nd	3,000	
3rd	2,000	
4th	1,000	

Memoirs de l'Academie des Inscript. tom. 31. p. 254.
The Baga Vedan counts thus,

1st age	4,800	years

2nd	3,600
3rd	2,400
4th	<u>1,200</u>
Total	12,000

The Indians figured this system by a cow with four legs; or the number twelve, taken successively four times.

Another Indian period establishes the duration of the world thus,

1st age	1,728,000	years
2nd	1,296,000	
3rd	864,000	
4th	<u>432,000</u>	
Total	4,320,000	

Now the smallest of these numbers (432,000) elevated to 2, 3, and 4, will give a sum total of 4,320,000.

The Indians say that the year of the gods is composed of 360 years of those of men; if you divide 4,320,000 for 360 you will have 12.

In the Chaldean period, as given by Berosus, we find the same numbers of 432,000, and to compose it, he follows the arithmetic order, thus:

1st degree	12,000
2nd	24,000
3rd	36,000
4th	48,000
5th	60,000

Mr. Hutchinson has proved, that the globes, on the top of the two columns, at the portico of the temple, were orreries, or mechanical representations of the motions of the heavenly bodies.[98]

I think, that after those circumstances, which afforded so many facilities for the introduction of the system of the Dionysian Artificers in Judea, the continuance of the same, in subsequent periods, cannot be of difficult explanation.

We find it stated, in the Book of the Maccabees,[99] that a society existed in those days in Judea, called the

6th	72,000
7th	84,000
8th	96,000
Total	432,000

[98] The columns or pillars were denominated יכיז {Hebrew YKYZ} and werbeH} זעבB!Z} the first signifies establish, from זיכ {Hebrew KYZ} to establish or make firm; the second signifies in strength, from the proposition ב {Hebrew B} in, and the root זוע {Hebrew !WZ} strength.

[99] "Now the Assideans were the first amongst the children of Israel that sought peace of them."
Maccab. vii. v. 13.
I should translate this passage differently, thus:
"And those, who amongst the sons of Israel were called Assideans, were the first of this assembly, and they wished to ask them peace."
According to this interpretation, by far more expressive of the text, it is seen, that the Assideans were a respectable body, for they were the first of that assembly.
In I Maccab. ii. v. 42, it is said, "Then came there unto him a company of Assideans, who were mighty men of Israel, even all such as were voluntarily devoted unto the law."
The very word Assidean or Cassidean is supposed to be derived from the Hebrew Cassidim, which in Psalm 78. v. 2. is taken in the sense of men pious, holy, full of piety and mercy.

Assideans or Cassideans, whose business it was to take care of the repairs of the temple.

From these Cassideans proceeded the sect or society of the Essenians, which, according to Philo and Josephus, were the same as the Assideans; and probably, because they admitted no women in their assemblies, Pliny says[100] that they were propagated without wives.

Josephus[101] mentions the first of the Essenians, in the time of Aristobulus, and Antigonus the son of Hircanus; but Suidas[102] and others were of opinion that they were a branch of the Rechabites, who subsisted before the captivity.

Josephus, probably ignorant of the secret tenets of the Essenians, also accuses them of worshipping the sun, or saying prayers before the sun rising, as if to incite him to rise. But this very accusation, again, identifies them with the sect of the Dionysian Artificers, who, as appears by the reasons above stated, were supposed to adore the sun.

Josephus relates many other particulars, by which, in a striking manner, he brings them to what we have related of the other societies which preceded them.[103] It also points out the conformity of their ideas with those of the Platonists

---

[100] "So for thousands of centuries, incredible to be said, this people is eternal, without any body being born amongst them."
Pliny, Lib. V. cap. 17.

[101] Josephus, Lib. 13. cap. 19.

[102] in προγονοι {Greek *progonoi*}.

[103] "Before they admit any one who desire it, into their sect, they put him to one year's probation, and inure him to the practice of their most uneasy exercises. After this term they admit him into the common refectory, and the place where they bathe; but not into the interior of the house, till after another trial of two years; then they are allowed to make a kind of profession, wherein they engage by horrible oaths, to observe the laws of piety, justice, and modesty; fidelity to God and their Prince; never to discover the secrets of their sect to strangers, and to preserve the books of their masters, and the names of angels with great care."
Josephus, loco citato.

and Dionysians, on the nature of the soul.[104] In short, they used symbols, allegories, and parables, after the manner of the ancients.[105]

The practices of those Essenians are represented by Philo[106] as the most pacific, and full of social virtues; and those amongst them who were most enthusiastic for their tenets, had their goods in common, as the Christians had in the first ages of Christianity.[107]

The Essenians had not their ceremonies and mysteries, recorded in history; but thus far we know, that they transmitted to posterity the doctrines which they received from their ancestors;[108] they had also distinguishing

---

[104] "They hold the soul to be immortal, and believe that souls descend from the highest air into the bodies animated by them, whither they are drawn by some natural attraction, which they cannot resist; and after death, they swiftly return to the place, from whence they came, as if freed from a long and melancholy captivity. In respect to the state of the soul after death, they have almost the same sentiments as the heathen, who place the souls of good men in the Elysian fields, and those of the wicked in Tartarus."
Josephus, loco citato.

[105] Philo, Lib. V. cap. 17.

[106] Some employ themselves in husbandry, others in trade and manufactures of such things only as are useful in time of peace, their designs being beneficial only to themselves and other men . . . . ."
"You do not find an artificer among them, who would make an arrow, a dart, or sword, or helmet, or cuirass, or shield, or any sort of arms, machines, or warlike instruments."
Philo, loco citato.

[107] "Their instructions run principally on holiness, equity, justice, economy, policy, the distinction between real good and real evil; of what is indifferent, what we ought to pursue or to avoid. The three fundamental maxims of their morality are, the love of God, of virtue, and of our neighbour."
Philo, loco citato.

[108] "the Essenians transmitted the doctrines they had received from their ancestors."
Philo. De vita contemplativa
Apud opera, p. 691

signs;[109] and the festival banquets;[110] though it does not appear that they followed the profession of builders or architects exclusively.

Out of Judea we find also societies distinguished by the same characters as the Essenians, and with the same tenets of Plato; for, the Pythagoreans also employed the symbols from the art of building. [111]

The Dionysian Artificers existed also in Syria, Persia, and India; [112] and the Eleusinian mysteries were preserved in Europe, even at Rome, until the eighth century of the Christian era. [113]

After this epoch, Europe was visited by the most barbarous nations who, persecuting every scientific research, scattered a general darkness, in which all the labours of the ancients, in favor of mankind, were nearly lost, in the general ignorance of their times.

Those very societies and sects, had also been in former periods much abused, and the ceremonies converted, as we have seen, for the worst of purposes: this was another powerful cause for their decline and ruin.

Christianity was then in Europe, the only bond of morality, by which power could, in some measure, be controuled, or restrained.

When the sciences began to revive, a general fanaticism prevailed, and a spirit of persecution appeared, which caused the ancient doctrines of philosophers, and the

---

[109] "They had distinguishing signs."
Ib.
[110] "I shall say something of their congregations and how often they celebrated their banquets, &c."
Ib. p. 692.
[111] Vide Iamblicus, de Vita Pythagoræ, cap. 17. and Basnage, History of the Jews, B. II. cap. 13.
[112] Strabo, p. 471.
[113] Psellus, quoted by Clinch, Antologia Hibernica, for January, 1794.

old systems of morality to be regarded only as offsprings of atheism, and practices of idolatry.

Under these circumstances, the Eleusinians, the Dionysian Artificers, Assideans or Essenians, sunk into such oblivion, that no mention is made of them in history.

In the tenth century, during the wars of the crusades, some societies were instituted in Palestine, and Europe, which adopted some regulations resembling those of the ancient fraternities. But is was in England, and chiefly in Scotland, where the remains of the old system, identified with that of the Dionysian Artificers, were discovered in modern times.

Cætera desunt.